Pebble® Plus

Cool Robots

TINY ROBOTS

by Kathryn Clay

Consulting Editor: Gail Saunders-Smith, PhD

Consultant: Seth Hutchinson, PhD
Department of Electrical and Computer Engineering
University of Illinois

CAPSTONE PRESS
a capstone imprint

Pebble Plus is published by Capstone Press,
1710 Roe Crest Drive, North Mankato, Minnesota 56003
www.capstonepub.com

Library of Congress Cataloging-in-Publication Data
Clay, Kathryn, author.
 Tiny robots / Kathryn Clay.
     pages cm.—(Pebble plus) (Cool robots)
 Summary: "Tiny robots include everything from a climbing microbot to a nanobot that goes inside the human body. Find out just what these awesome machines can do."—Provided by publisher.
 Includes bibliographical references and index.
  ISBN 978-1-4914-0587-1 (hb)—ISBN 978-1-4914-0651-9 (pb)— ISBN 978-1-4914-0621-2 (eb)
1. Robotics—Juvenile literature. 2. Nanoscience—Juvenile literature. 3. Nanotechnology—Juvenile literature. 4. Technological innovations—Juvenile literature. I. Title.
 TJ211.2.R557 2015
 629.8'92—dc23   2014002309

Editorial Credits
Erika L. Shores, editor; Terri Poburka, designer; Katy LaVigne, production specialist

Photo Credits
Getty Images: Photo Researchers/Hank Morgan, 5, Stone/Coneyl Jay, 15, Win McNamee, 21; Harvard School of Engineering and Applied Sciences/Kevin Ma and Pakpong Chirarattananon, 19; Institute of Robotics and Intelligent Systems, ETH Zurich, 11 (both); Kyodo via AP Images, 9; Photo by the Self-organizing Systems Research group at Harvard University, 13; Photo courtesy Mike Shores, 7; SuperStock: F1 ONLINE/RED, cover; *The Christian Science Monitor* via Getty Images: Tony Avelar, 17

Design Elements
Shutterstock: Irena Peziene, Kate Pru

Note to Parents and Teachers

The Cool Robots set supports national science standards related to science, technology, engineering, and mathematics. This book describes and illustrates tiny robots. The images support early readers in understanding the text. The repetition of words and phrases helps early readers learn new words. This book also introduces early readers to subject-specific vocabulary words, which are defined in the Glossary section. Early readers may need assistance to read some words and to use the Table of Contents, Glossary, Read More, Internet Sites, and Index sections of the book.

Printed in China
032014   008085LEOF14

Table of Contents

Mighty Bots

Some mighty machines are small enough to fit on a fingertip. Scientists build tiny robots to do all kinds of work.

Microbots

Hexbug Nano V2 is a microbot.

It moves like a real bug.

The V2's tiny legs help

it climb up tubes.

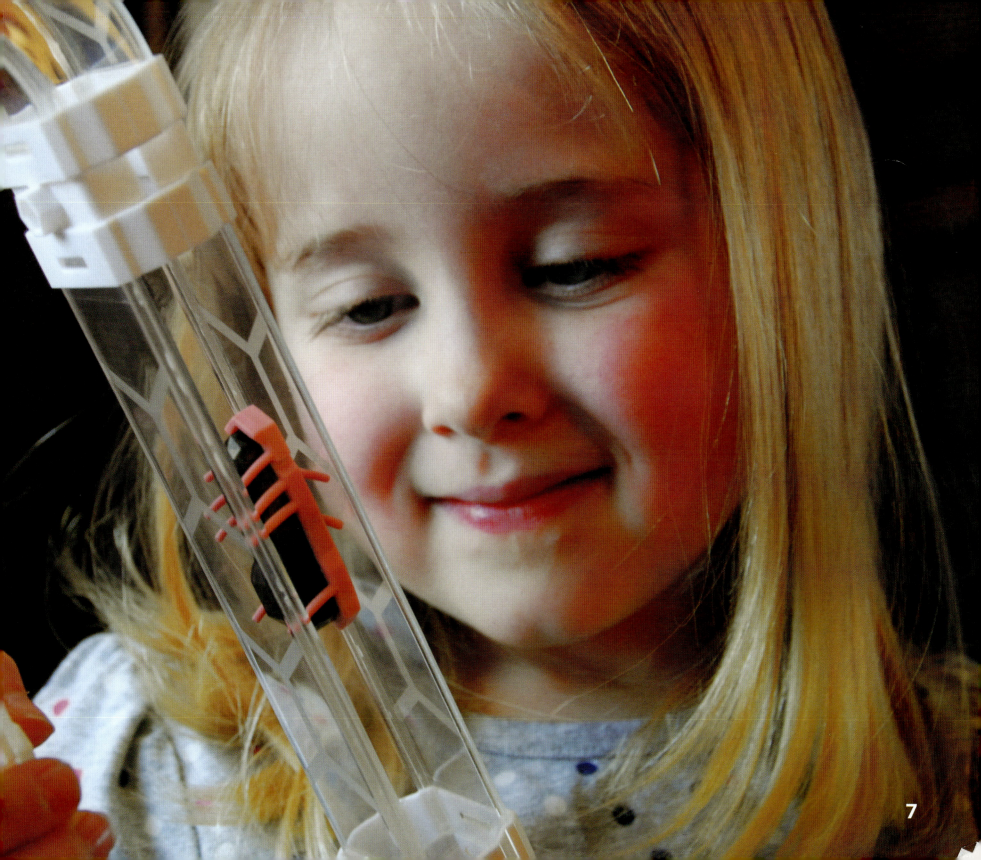

People might swallow robots in the future. Scientists made a pill-size robot. The robot takes pictures inside a person's body.

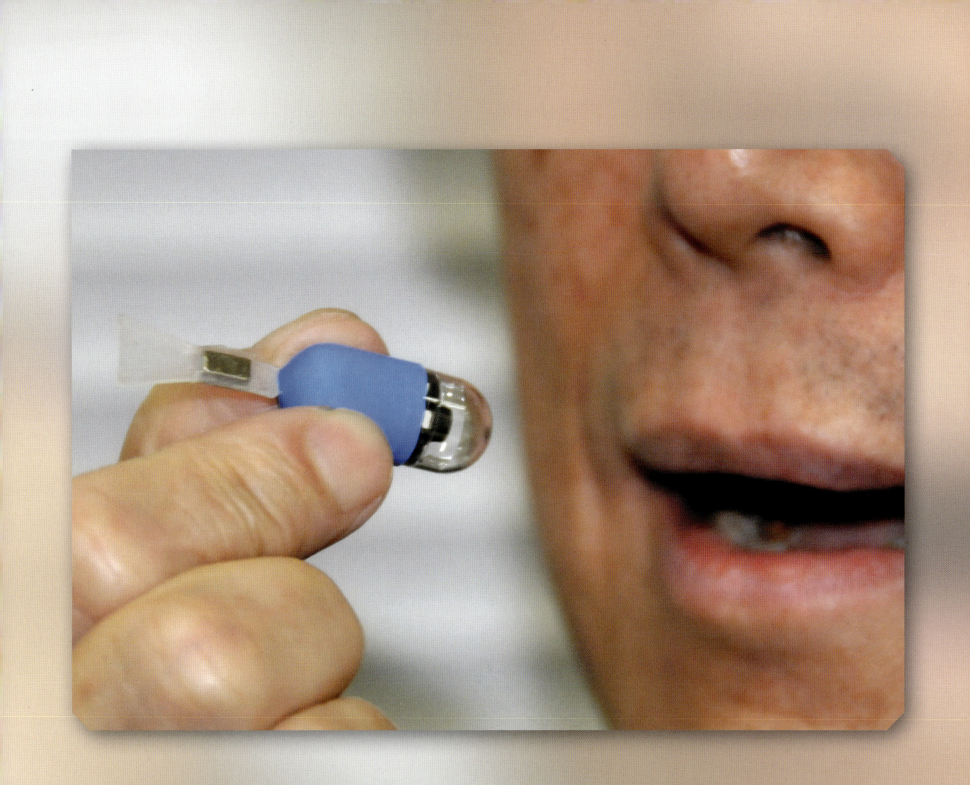

Eye surgeons hope to use microbots one day. The OctoMag uses magnets to move a microbot into the eye.

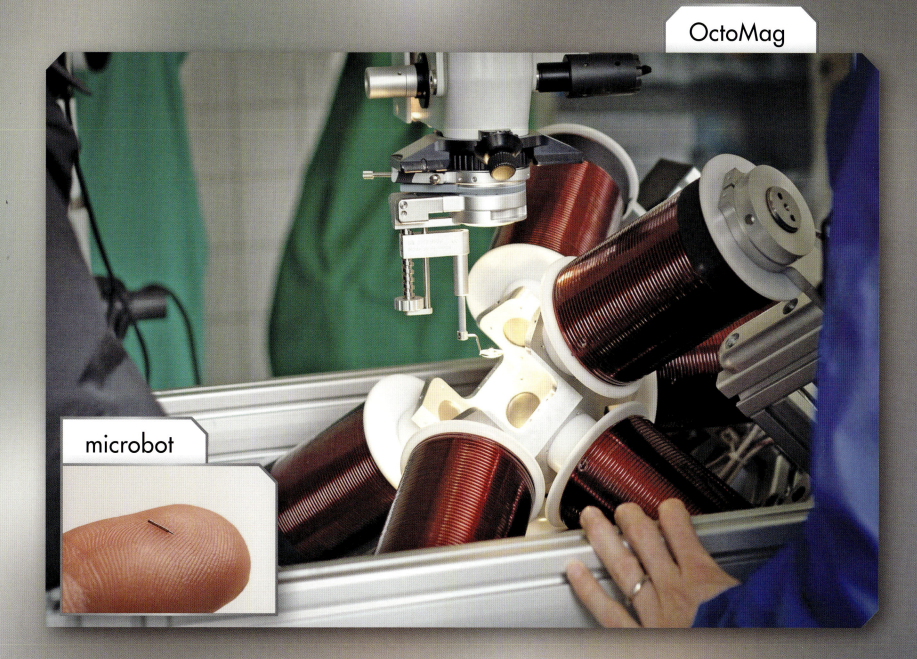

microbot

Kilobots light up and vibrate.
The lights and sounds let
these small robots "talk"
to each other.

Nanobots

Nanobots are too small to see. Someday doctors might place nanobots inside people. The tiny robots could fight diseases.

Illustration of future nanobot and blood cells

Mini Flyers

Four spinning blades lift quadrotors into the air. These robots could fly into damaged buildings and send back pictures.

RoboBee is the size of a penny.

It weighs less than a stamp.

Thin wings flap 120 times

each second.

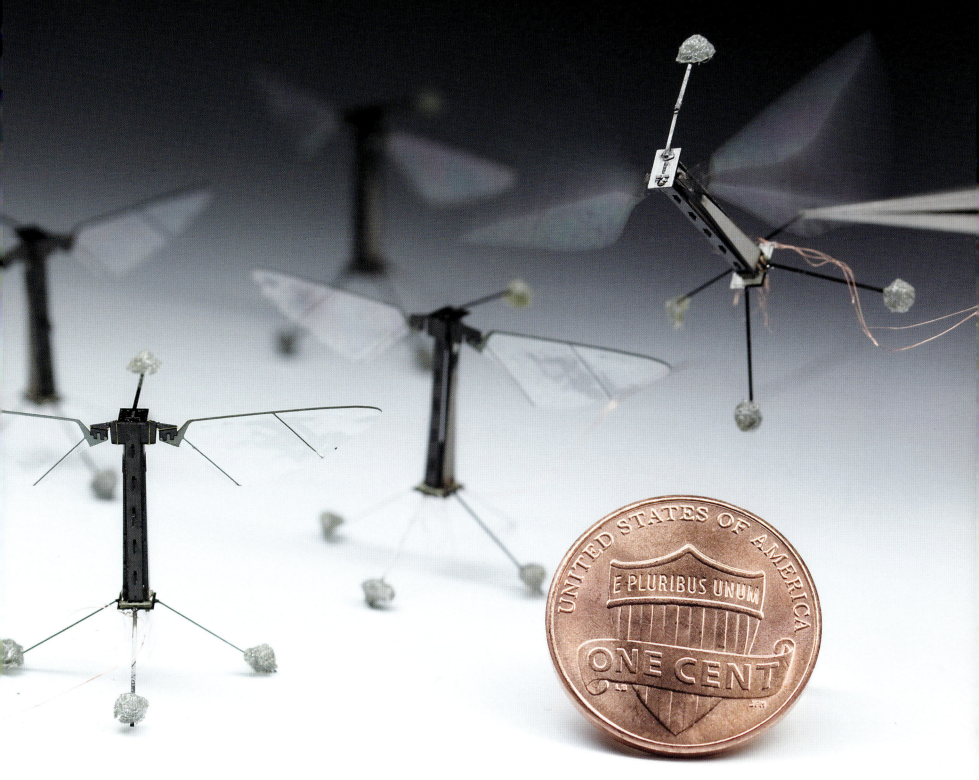

Samarai Flyer moves like a maple seed. The robot is tossed into the air or takes off from the ground. Its wing moves in a spiral.

Glossary

disease—a sickness or illness

magnet—a piece of metal that pulls objects made of iron or steel toward it

robot—a machine that can do work and is operated by remote control or a computer

spiral—a pattern that goes around in circles

vibrate—to move back and forth quickly

Read More

Hyland, Tony. *Robot World.* Fast Facts. Mankato, Minn.: Sea-to-Sea Publications, 2012.

Rau, Dana Meachen. *Robots.* Surprising Science. New York: Marshall Cavendish Benchmark, 2011.

Internet Sites

FactHound offers a safe, fun way to find Internet sites related to this book. All of the sites on FactHound have been researched by our staff.

Here's all you do:

Visit *www.facthound.com*

Type in this code: 9781491405871

Super-cool stuff! Check out projects, games and lots more at **www.capstonekids.com**

Critical Thinking Using the Common Core

1. Describe some of the things tiny robots can do that people can't. (Key Ideas and Details)

2. Look at the picture on page 15. How does it help you understand how a nanobot might fight diseases? (Integration of Knowledge and Details)

Index

Word Count: 183
Grade: 1
Early-Intervention Level: 18